NO CHECKMATE

MONTESSORI CHESS LESSONS
FOR AGE 3 TO 90+

SUSAN MAYCLIN STEPHENSON

Also by Susan Mayclin Stephenson

The Joyful Child:
Montessori, Global Wisdom
for Birth to Three

Child of the World:
Montessori, Global Education
for Age 3-12+

The Universal Child, Guided by Nature:
Adaptation of the
2013 International Congress
Presentation

NO CHECKMATE
Montessori Chess Lessons for Age 3 to 90+
Copyright © 2016 Susan Mayclin Stephenson

FIRST EDITION

Michael Olaf Montessori Company
PO Box 1162
Arcata, CA 95518, USA
www.michaelolaf.net
michaelolafcompany@gmail.com

For translation and foreign publishing rights contact: michaelolafbooks@gmail.com

ISBN 978-1-879264-18-2
ISBN 1-879264-18-8

Cover: An image of mixed media art by the author
"Exploring a Traditional Chinese Chess Set with Pagodas for Castles"

Illustrations: By the author and friends

Printed in the United States of America

CONTENTS

HOW CHESS BECAME
A WHOLE FAMILY GAME

Chess was not part of my experience as a child. But as I traveled around the world through Europe, the Middle East, and Asia as a college sophomore, I could see that I had missed something. I was one of a group of students and professors traveling together on the first experimental college semester on a ship. Everywhere we went people who could not even speak the same language could play chess together! I was determined to learn the game and bought my first chess set in Hong Kong.

To this day I am still not interested in becoming an expert chess player, but it has certainly opened doors for me during travels. Because I am a Montessori teacher, an artist, and a person interested in learning about the cultures of the world, the beauty of chess sets themselves, and the fascinating history of the game have drawn me further and further into this realm. Shortly after learning chess myself I began to teach children. This is not a book only about chess; it is about children. It is about sharing our lives, our interests and passions, with our children.

It was 1968 and my first child, Narda, was three years old. Whenever I played chess with a friend or her father, I would let her play with the chess pieces that had been removed from the board. She marched them around the table, gave them names and acted out make-believe scenarios of everyday life with them. She seemed content, but never for very long. I could tell she was curious about what we adults were doing with this board and the pieces. She seemed to want to know what was so important about a chess set that engaged us for so long, but I had no idea of how to involve her in the playing of real chess. And after all she was just a three-year-old child, and was supposed to be interested only in playing with dolls, right?

I was wrong about that. We enrolled Narda in a Montessori school in San Francisco in 1969. We were so impressed by the results of this experience for her, the whole family moved to London, England in1970 so that I could take my first of three yearlong AMI Montessori teacher-training courses.

During that year my eyes were opened to the amazing potential of a child from the age of 2.5 to 7. In 1971 we were back in San Francisco. I was teaching at the same Montessori school in San Francisco where Narda had begun at age 3. She was now 5 years old and I knew that the first six years were the most important time to teach language—especially the language of the child's environment that in this case included the language of chess—and the attitudes, manners, and daily activities of the family. So we began to teach her chess, and to my surprise her little sister Ursula who was only 3 years old also wanted to learn. Why not? I began to apply the Montessori principles I had learned, to analyze the game in order to make it palatable, understandable, and enjoyable by young children. Over the years I have repeated these lessons, often changing to reflect what I learned from individual children; I have taught chess to all 3 of my children, 4 grandchildren, and many others in Montessori primary and elementary classes. As the writing of this book progresses, I have been told by many people that they want a copy when it is finished. These people want to learn an interesting and culturally significant game in a cooperative, non-competitive way. That is the Montessori way of learning.

How did I write this book? With a lot of help from friends and family. Even though I have taught young children how to play chess for many years, it was quite a challenge to write down how this happens. Several times, after describing the stages for learning how the pieces move, I asked friends to try to try to follow these directions to see if they actually made sense, to see if they could be followed by an adult who was preparing to teach chess to a child.

One woman, while taking turns with me as we moved a bishop several times around the board, practicing the ways a bishop could move, kept saying, "What's the Point?" In her mind the main goal of chess is to win, to compete. She did not know how to play chess, but she knew enough about chess and games in general to automatically be thinking "winner" and "loser", and not just gently moving chess pieces around on the board as though they were taking a Sunday walk in a park.

To explain, I used the example of washing dishes. In the very first *casa dei bambini* (house of children) in the San Lorenzo slums of Rome, which was an experiment by the first female medical doctor in Italy to test the methods she has used with "untrainable" children, the lab class was outfitted with the usual children's toys of the day, and an adult did the cooking, serving, washing dishes, cleaning, etc. Very soon the children, who were around 3-6 years of age, asked if they could do the work that they saw going on around them. Once they were given real cleaning materials made to fit their hands and bodies, and were shown how to do the work, they always chose what was to become known as *practical life* activities. They no longer were interested in make-believe and playing with toys. This real work is called "practical life" work and it is still the most popular work in Montessori classrooms around the world today.

But the point of this work of washing dishes is very different for an adult than for a child. When an adult sets out to wash dishes, for example, the goal is to get the dishes as clean as possible in the shortest amount of time. Not so for a child.

The child wants to get his hands on real tools, and to do what he has seen others do. He might spend 20 minutes washing one plate. He might wash and then rinse and then wash and rinse the same plate over and over. He might really get the food off of the plate and he might not. But that is not "the point." He is not just taking care of the dishes; he is constructing his brain, his body, and his whole self.

When one analyzes the steps necessary to do dish washing in the Montessori classroom, one looks at all of the skills necessary before this can be attempted, and then prepares the child by teaching him how to, for example, turn the water tap on and off, fill a bucket of water and carry it, carry a ceramic plate carefully without dropping it, stack the plates carefully in a dish drainer without breaking them (no plastic plates are found in a Montessori classroom or these activities would not be a challenge), squeeze just a small amount of dish soap into the basin, put on and fasten an apron, clean up water spills with a mop, and much more. Think of what is going on in the brain of a child as he decides to do these things in a logical order. What good would it do to put on the apron after the work is finished for example, or to squeeze in the dish soap after the dishes are washed? This is high-level mental work for a child at this age.

So it is with chess. This is a complicated game even in the beginning when the child is just learning the rules of movements of the various pieces. But the child is learning a lot that has nothing to do with competition or winning. He is learning how to handle chess pieces carefully, how to take turns, how to wait, how to politely finish a game, how to do things in a logical order, and most of all, he is getting to do things, real things, that he has seen adults and older children do and by doing so he feels included in the life of his family and school.

A BRIEF INTRODUCTION TO MONTESSORI

The Montessori method and chess?

Maria Montessori was the first woman physician in Italy. She did not plan to create a way of educating children, but her methods of observation, learning about children, and following where they led her have, for over 100 years, been a revolution in the way we look at the potential of the human being. I hope you will be inspired to read more about this amazing woman who finally realized that with this method we can discover the true road to personal thriving, and peace among peoples and nations.

One may well ask, what do learning chess, a historically competitive game based on war strategies, have to do with Montessori, a system of raising and educating children that is compassionate and cooperative, the antithesis of war. I hope by the end of this book you will have formed your own answer to this question.

One of my goals is to show that one can excel without competing, that a person can learn to think and plan and prepare for the unexpected, without needing extrinsic rewards such as gold stars, verbal praise, or fame and fortune. This has been proven for over 100 years all over the world. The Montessori method prepares student to succeed. in Montessori environments and I hope that this combination of learning chess and using Montessori ideas will inspire adults to go further in the area of learning cooperatively.

Planes of development

The applications of the lessons in this book depend on the age and stage of development of the child or student. A 2-year-old will be attracted in a way that is very different than a 7-year-old or an adult. It is certainly not important for everyone to learn chess, but it is not a good feeling for anyone to think that they are not smart enough to learn chess and this is not uncommon. Just as math and geometry have been analyzed and taught in such a way in Montessori environments that they are enjoyed and understood by all, so can chess be. There are two basic things I have learned in the process of teaching chess. The first is that children want to do what their adults are doing: they will always choose "real" activities over most toys if given the chance. The second is that almost anything can be taught at any age if one has knowledge of the needs and the developmental stages of the student, the skill at the thing to be taught, and—most of all—an understanding of how to put the student and the skill in touch with each other. This last quality is known in Montessori circles as, "The Art of Teaching."

Although Montessori is thought by many to be a pre-school to prepare children academically for real school this is far from accurate. The essence of Montessori is to discover and to support the best in the natural development of humans from birth through old age. There are programs that teach parents how to prepare the Montessori environment in the home in preparation for a birth, elementary, middle, and high schools, and programs to help elders with dementia be as independent and happy as possible.

Human needs and tendencies

One of the areas of Montessori philosophy that one learns about during teacher training is called, "Human Needs and Tendencies." Montessori describes each of these tendencies as a life force or natural guide which drive humans at all ages toward physical, mental, and spiritual development and fulfillment. The list among Montessorians is fluid but always include the following: exploration, order, orientation, communication, movement, work, repetition, exactness, abstraction, and perfection. But how these tendencies show themselves depends on the stage of development, or the plane of development, of the human. For example consider exploration. In the first plane (the first 6 years), exploration is mostly done by the physical senses — hearing, touching, tasting, seeing, and smelling. In the second stage, 6-12 years, the exploration is done more with the mind, reaching back into history and far into space, and in learning to get along with and work with others. In the third plane, ages 12-18, the child explores with emotions and again with the senses and with the mind, discovering his own learning styles, time management methods, and responsibilities and joys, and this continues throughout life.

So in teaching chess we have to consider this. The 0-6 child wants to touch and see and move the chess pieces. The 6-12 child wants to explore where chess came from and why the rules are the way they are. The adolescent and adult wants to know that he is indeed capable of learning chess, and discover his own way of learning chess and playing the game in the wider society.

The absorbent mind

It is well known that a person can easily learn a second language, or a third, or more, in the first 6 years of life, and that it takes a lot more effort to do this as an adult. This is because a child in the first 6 years of life has what is called in the Montessori field an absorbent mind. During this time the child takes in everything that is in the environment, good and bad, without effort, like a sponge soaking up water.

From birth on, when many people think he is only eating and sleeping, the child will be watching and listening and learning what it means to be the kind of human he will grow up to be in his particular family, neighborhood, and culture. Therefore, the adult is the most important learning "material" in his environment. This is why I stress in this book the many polite and thoughtful details for the adult to model as he teaches chess to the very young.

A BRIEF INTRODUCTION TO CHESS
AND HOW TO USE THIS BOOK

The beginnings of chess are shrouded in mystery and the game has changed many times throughout history. But the basic agreement today is that there are two teams or armies and they are at war with each other. If the king is captured the battle is lost. This war takes place on the chess board with 64 squares. The squares are light and dark but they are always called white and black. The board is always placed so that there is a white square in the right hand corner nearest each player. There are eight ranks or rows that are horizontal, and 8 files that are the vertical rows up and down the board. There are 6 different kinds of pieces: king (one white and one black), queen (one white and one black), bishops (two of each color), knights (two of each color), rooks or castles (two of each color), pawns (8 of each color). There is an ongoing debate about whether or not it is correct to call a "rook" a "castle" but I have always done so because it makes sense to see the castle turrets on the traditional chess piece. You can use either rook or castle, but be consistent from the beginning.

Each of these pieces has a unique way of moving. Learning the names of the pieces and the rules for how they move is the essence of this book.

This book is called "No Checkmate" because the intention is to take one up to the point of competition, winning, and "checkmate." There are plenty of books that teach how to win, how to beat another person. There are many, many books on how to play the traditional win/lose game, some written for children, some for adults. And then many more on the theory and tactics of chess and even records of famous games played throughout history. Please go to your library or bookstore for these. In the next chapter you can learn a bit about the game beyond the focus of this book.

In this Montessori introduction the point is to learn the basic moves of each piece, practice working together with another person to move the pieces around on the board in the correct fashion, and to get a taste of how playing with another person can be cooperative, joyful, and kind.

In this Montessori way of teaching chess we speak of "three levels of games" from learning about the individual pieces, to actually beginning to play a competitive game and trying to win or get one's chess partner in check.

Forget everything you might know about playing chess. Just think about relaxing and spending enjoyable time with your child and helping him learn to enjoy chess.

For anyone who has learned chess the usual way, the following carefully analyzed steps might seem tedious and overly detailed. But it is just because the process is broken down into small steps that this method meets the needs of the young child. At this age repetition is very important. Logical steps that are repeated with each piece are very satisfying to the child's need for order. Emphasis on the care of placing the pieces in the exact center of a square satisfies a child's desire to practice the skill of moving his hands and fingers in ways that are a challenge and can lead to perfection in movement. All of the details included in these first lessons have a purpose. All are based on experience with young children in Montessori environments, home and school. And I should add that many adults, who had previously thought that chess was just too difficult to put forth the effort to learn, have really enjoyed learning in this way, even if they had no intention of teaching a child. So I hope you will also enjoy seeing the Montessori way of teaching, not just teaching chess, as having many layers of value.

The actions of the adult are the most powerful lessons. Being relaxed, letting go of the traditional way of competing in games, and either speaking OR moving a piece, not both at the same time.

This is one important bit of Montessori wisdom to share with you before beginning the lessons. The child will be able to LISTEN carefully or WATCH carefully. NOT BOTH AT THE SAME TIME. This is something all Montessori teachers practice for hours as they give lessons to each other during a Montessori teacher's course. Even if you will be practicing the following lessons alone, or with another adult, you should practice this technique, because then it will become a habit and increase the likelihood of success in teaching chess to a young child.

During AMI (Association Montessori Internationale) teacher training courses the trainer first demonstrates the lesson or activity, carefully moving the materials and carrying out the steps, in the correct order. She gives a detailed explanation of the material, explains the indirect and direct preparation that come before this lesson, the age range of the child, parallel activities in other areas of the curriculum, the exact steps for the lesson, the accompanying language, variations of the basic lessons, and applying this concept to the wider environment such as the classroom. Students watch carefully, recording what they see and hear. Then they participate in many hours of required "practicals" where they practice giving these lessons to each other. In my own teacher-training courses, I found that taking notes instead of being given printouts of lessons, and the many hours of practice giving lessons to other adults were extremely valuable. We could find out what we might have left out, or described incorrectly, during our note taking. It was and is so important to discover these things before attempting to give a lesson to a child!

With this book I suggest that one goes through similar steps. First you can look at the directions, taking notes or drawing pictures if that is your way of learning, and try to follow the steps with a chessboard and pieces. You might want to ask a friend to read the directions to you as you follow them using the chess pieces and board.

Then try to teach another adult. If you are going to be teaching a child under the age of seven years it is helpful to know that from birth to seven is the period of the absorbent mind, when children take in every detail of what they experience. So you do not want to be making corrections in your lessons when teaching a child of this age. Practice, practice, practice. I remember hearing about a lesson a teacher gave on the pink tower which is a set of ten pink cubes that are stacked very carefully on top of each other from the largest to the smallest. One tries to place them so they are exactly in the center of the cube beneath, without having to adjust. It is obvious to the child watching the lesson that this takes concentration and controlled movement. As the teacher in this case finished carefully placing each cube she quietly said to herself, "There" as though to express relief that she had placed the cube correctly. Later she noticed the child doing the work on his own. Each time he placed a cube he said, "There." That's the absorbent mind at work.

Keep this in mind as you practice the lessons in this book on your own, and with other adults, before teaching a child. This kind of attention and focus is one of the great attractions of Montessori education and it is as valuable to the teacher as to the student because it keeps us in the present moment and adds elegance and care to our daily lives.

CHESS GRACE AND COURTESY

Graceful movement and balance of the whole body

At around 1.5 years of age a child, so glad to be in an upright position with hands free, wants to put forth as much effort as possible and delights in carrying heavy things. This practice solidifies the balance of walking, carrying something, and watching where one is going. One of the first things you might offer a child in the learning of chess might be the opportunity to carry the chess set to the table, placing it quietly on the table, and putting it away when the game, between two other people, is finished.

Graceful movement of the hands, and eye-hand control

Eye-hand control, or the ability of the hand to do what the brain tells it to do, is the next challenge that children love and many examples are given in Montessori communities for children from infancy to 7 years. Eye-hand control means moving something with one's hand in the way the brain directs. Examples include pouring water from a pitcher into a glass, or placing an object on a surface exactly where it is wanted without having to move or adjust the placement afterward. In chess this skill can be practiced by the placing of the chessboard on the table, placing the chess pieces on the table, placing the pieces exactly in the center of each square on the board during a game, and carefully putting them back in the box or container when the game is over.

I know that to a person unfamiliar to Montessori education this emphasis on detail can sound boring and tedious, but it has been shown all over the world for over 100 years that children want this. They love a challenge of movement and sometimes will repeat an activity, unasked, over and over again until they master it to their satisfaction. The more detailed and exacting the movement challenge the better for the child's brain, body, and spirit. Today the connection of the brain and body in very young children is being studied and appreciated by neuroscientists and because of the way

Montessori provides these challenges for children Montessori education is being sought after on a new level

The courtesy of shaking hands

When a child enters a Montessori class, at least in Western Cultures, the first thing he usually does is shake hands with the teacher who is sitting on a chair just inside the classroom so her face is at the child's level.

This marks the beginning of the child's day at school; it sets the energy of mutual respect and focus on being in the moment. Similarly you can teach this in chess. Either person can offer to shake hands at the beginning of a game or lesson.

But the main reason for this is because the manners of chess require that at the end of a game the two people shake hands and say something along the lines of, "Thank you for playing chess with me," or, "I enjoyed playing chess with you." This may not seem like a very important step in the beginning of learning to play chess, but it is extremely helpful when, at the 3rd level of chess, both people are trying to win, and someone loses. Knowing that one is going to end the game in such a polite manner can prevent the frustration, anger, and ill manners that are sometimes displayed when a person (even adults) lose a game.

One day I was giving a chess lesson to my grandson who was 4 years old. His little sister, age 2, seemed to be slightly interested but not yet ready for the stages her brother was ready for. Even though I invited her to participate, this two-year-old really could not fathom the idea that she will someday be older and more capable, able to do things her older brother can do. So she was feigning disinterest and sort of watching out of the corner of her eye as the lesson progressed and we ended the game by shaking hands and saying polite things. As the game ended I invited her to take on the job of carefully returning the pieces to the box. However a few hours later, when her father arrived, she met him with these words in a very excited voice, "Papa, when a chess game is over we shake hands and say, 'Thank you for playing chess with me!' Hold out your hand and I'll show you!"

Perhaps because of the security of knowing how a game ends, she became very interested in learning more. She wanted to practice putting the pawns very carefully in the middle of each square of the board, and placing them very carefully back in the box at the end of our very short game. She was NOT interested in learning to move the pieces. That was all right. I followed her lead and she felt that putting the pieces on the board and then putting them away was a real game. And a real game it was. But what she loved most of all was the shaking hand at the end of the game and saying, "Thank you for playing chess with me!"

The courtesy of patiently watching and waiting one's turn

Very young children are often thought to be ruled by impulse and lacking self-control. Some impulses are very valuable. For example if we watch carefully and provide the supportive environment where the adult is skilled in observing, children from birth will sleep the proper amount of time, eat the proper amount of food, and exercise their bodies in the correct manner. But there are impulses that are not always socially acceptable, such as a child naturally wanting to touch everything in sight.

This is an important and valuable way of learning about the world, but not in the wrong places, such as a grocery store where everything on the lower shelves would end up on the floor.

Self-control is the ability to control one's actions in the face of temptations. It is the process of regulating one's behavior, or delaying gratification, in order to achieve goals. In the Montessori 0-7 environment there is only one set of each kind of materials. One pink tower, one shoe polishing activity, one set of color pencils for drawing, one set up for washing dishes, or doing long division on a bead frame, etc. A child is allowed to choose anything he knows how to use correctly (he would have learned from a lesson by the teacher, another child, or by watching someone) and to use it without time limit, as long as he is using it correctly, which means that he is learning the information imparted from that activity or piece of material. He is not asked to share, or to put it away because someone else is waiting. All children in a Montessori environment learn to respect and not interrupt someone who is concentrating deeply in working on a particular piece of material. Today we call this "delayed gratification" and it is one of the mental abilities measured to track a child's development. Children learn very early that the rule is one can work with any of the materials he has chosen until he is finished and then it will be put back on the shelf and another child can work with it. This is a wonderful example of a child controlling his urge to touch everything he sees because he learns that he will have a chance later.

In the beginning chess lessons, a young child will often have trouble waiting while his chess partner (or teacher) takes his turn. And so we give a lesson on "waiting your turn." We can teach this by demonstrating for a child how we put our hands together in our lap when it is the other person's turn, emphasizing that we are being silent and watching. This gives him something to master and to focus on as he waits.

Here is a story to illustrate how one child learned self-control. I was substitute teaching in a 2-6 Montessori class. There were a few children who were interrupting the work of others instead of finding something of their own to work on. I gathered these children, invited them to sit on the floor with me, and asked if they would like a lesson on, "Watching a friend work without interrupting." Of course they all said they would. Together we looked around the room to see if some of the children were working on their own. Identifying one child who was working at a table and concentrating, I said to the group in a very quiet voice, "First I am going to watch David work, and then you can have a turn to watch someone if you like."

I picked up a chair and carried it close to the table where David was working. Holding the chair in my hands, I then slowly took three steps backward, pausing between each step. I sat down on the chair and placed my hands in front of my mouth to show that my mouth was closed and I was not going to talk. Then I put my hands in my lap and watched David. After a few minutes I took the chair back to the place it had been originally, walked back to the group of children waiting for me, and invited a child to do the activity while we watched.

A week later I was in our public library and on the far side of the lobby was one of the children who had been in the group where I gave the "watching" lesson.

He took one look at me and ran across the lobby to a chair next to the magazine rack. He sat down on the chair, placed his hands in front of his mouth, and then in his lap, with the biggest smile on his face. The non-verbal communication was clear. He had learned the lesson and wanted me to show someone how well he could do this. We too often think children are not capable of doing certain things and maybe it is just because no one has carefully shown them how.

The courtesy of putting the chess set away

In the Montessori class it is the role of the adult to model not only constantly putting things away and tucking chairs or stools under a table and out of the way, but also to do so with a smile on our faces, and in such a careful way that children can emulate us when they are ready. The fact that there is always at least a 3-year age difference (at least above age 2.5 years) gives plenty of opportunity for the younger children to learn this from the older ones. At home it is much more difficult because parents have so many other things to take care of. But putting things away so they will be ready for the next person to use is a way of giving, and important for the child to learn. Sometimes, for the youngest child, the "putting away" is the most attractive part of the work so we should be ready for that. And completing a cycle of activity all the way to the end is very good for the brain. So model this and include the child whenever possible.

THREE LEVELS OF LEARNING CHESS, LEARNING WITHOUT COMPETING, THE LENGTH OF A GAME OR LESSON

Three levels of learning chess

This Montessori way of teaching chess has changed many times over the years as a result of observing different children at different ages. Dr. Montessori's message to us was, "Follow the Child," which means constant observation and adaptation of methods. Here are the three main levels of games that were eventually delineated and that have proved to be most helpful.

Level 1 – Learning the names of the pieces and their most basic moves

Level 2 – Playing a game where the adult teaches more about chess moves, both partners help each other to discover the best move, and the adult helps the child win the game.

Level 3 – Playing a game where both try to win

Learning without competing

Everyone who comes to understand this first level of learning chess thinks it makes sense to remove competition from learning. It is especially consistent with everything we do in the Montessori field. It is thought by many in the education world that competition against others is necessary for excellence. That we need the approval of others, gold stars, high grades, and so on to be thought successful, that we need to beat an adversary. One of the great discoveries in the Montessori educational world is that humans delight in working hard and doing their best, for no extrinsic reward, but rather for self satisfaction. In fact, learning for rewards and praise and winning can actually get in the way of the best efforts. In Montessori classes of all ages children are able to help and teach each other instead of competing with each other. Even though later on chess will probably become a competitive game, in these first years we stress that it is for spending time together and learning the beginning skills of the game.

The length of a game or lesson

How long each game takes depends on the interest of the child and it is always best to suggest an end to the game before he has become tired: "We have been playing this king game for a long time, you must be tired! Shall we put the pieces away? " The child is much more likely to want to continue if you have this attitude than if you try to lengthen the lesson by saying, "Come on, you can play one more game."

This last paragraph perhaps should be repeated over and over because it is applicable in everything one does, every lesson one gives, at home and in the classroom. I have often seen teachers walk up to a child and say, "You must find some work." Or "Why don't you do that again." Or in some other way give the message that what the child is doing is not good enough. When one sees a child wandering around or resting or spacing out, it is more successful to say, "Maybe you have done too much work this morning and you should have a rest." I have observed in many years in the classroom that the message received in this instance is that the child is working hard, is great just the way he is, and often, with this feeling of approval, will choose to continue with whatever he is working on.

If you don't quite understand what I am saying, then put yourself in the child's place. You have been weeding the garden and are lying on your back staring at the clouds. Your wife sees you and says, "You have not done very much weeding so I hope you finish the other raised bed before you stop for the day." Or she says, "Looks like you have worked pretty hard on that weeding, maybe you should take a break." Which comment is going to make you feel understood, and more likely to continue with your gardening?

NOT QUITE READY FOR LEVEL 1 GAMES?

Being included

All those years ago when I was trying out my new Montessori skills to begin to teach Narda how to play chess, it was clear that she was not really ready for the chess rules. I had shown her how the king moves and then how the queen moves. She was outraged! "If the Queen can go as far as she wants to any direction the king can too!" she told me. And so we played what I called "Narda's King Game," and I told her that it was fine to change the rules in games as long as everyone agreed on the changes at the beginning of the game.

Then, when it was Ursula's turn, same thing. Well, not exactly the same, but she didn't like the idea of pieces being all alone on the squares of the board and wanted them to be two pieces to a square. Fine. We played "Ursula chess games."

It was clear that sometimes a child is just not ready to learn the correct moves of chess pieces. But the child wants to be involved, to be included in the process. So the following are some ways that we have done this in our home. At the end of whichever of these games you might choose to do, you can show the child how to put the chess pieces away, and sometimes even shake hands and end with a polite, "Thank you. I enjoyed playing (or working) with you."

Setting up the furniture for a chess game

Instead of trying to force them to learn the regular rules I concentrated on other aspects of learning chess. We play chess on a low coffee table in front of the sofa in the living room these days. Sometimes an adult will choose to sit on the sofa and sometimes on a cushion on the floor. But because we have child-sized chairs in our home, one of the favorite chess preparation activities is for the very young child to carry the child's chair from the kitchen to the living room, and to put it back when the game is over. We have also given the task of getting the chess game out of the closet, carrying it carefully and placing it silently on the coffee table to the youngest child. These responsibilities, even if the game is going to be played between two older siblings or adults, gives him the feeling that he is indeed participating in the real life of the family, which young children want and need. This makes him feel necessary and helpful.

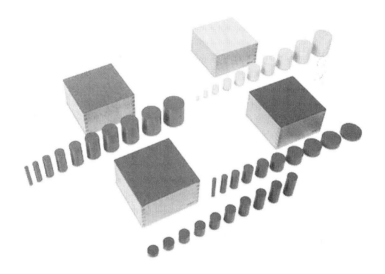

Handling the chess pieces

In the Montessori class the cylinder blocks and the knobless cylinders are always taught and used on a table, never on a floor or table mat. This is because carefully placing the thinnest cylinder would not be possible on a soft surface. It would fall over and the child would fail, making the work dissatisfying. As a result the careful and exact placing of all of the cylinders becomes meaningless and the activity is no longer an exercise in eye-hand control. It is the same with chess. A child wants to be challenged to do something that is not easy, and to feel himself improving. He does not want praise or rewards, but to feel the success from within, an intrinsic reward.

The chess game is carried out on a hard, flat surface for the same reason. When a child was not ready to learn the rules, he often was satisfied with his progress of handling the chess pieces. I challenged them to be able to put the pieces on the board so carefully that one could not hear a sound. We did the same thing putting them away. Sometimes a child will be satisfied with getting the chess pieces out of their box and placing them on the table next to the board, "without making a sound." Children at a very young age want to participate by doing the things they have seen their older siblings or parents do. That is the best way for them to learn.

Dusting or polishing chess pieces

This brings up a point that is sometimes misunderstood in a Montessori class. When a child asks if he can work with materials that he is not prepared for, for example wanting to get his hands on the beautiful glass beads that teach squaring and cubing before he has begun the basic math work the reply should never be, "No, you are not ready for that." The child doesn't understand that in time he will have the skills to work with more advanced materials, that someday he will be ready. He only hears the word, "NO!" Instead the teacher says, "Yes, you will be able to work with those materials, as soon as you can do this, and this, and this" perhaps pointing to the beginning shelves of math materials. "This one comes first. Would you like a lesson on that now?"

Sometimes, if a child is not even ready to begin the first math lesson and still wants to "work with" the beautiful bead materials, the teacher can say, "Yes, do you see that these beads and the shelves are really dusty? Would you like a lesson on dusting them?" Sometimes children have been able to practice their skill of wood polishing on materials in the Montessori classroom that they will not be using in the prescribed way until much later. This is all satisfying, important, real work.

In our home we have several chess sets from different countries. One of them is a set from India, with pieces carved into camels and elephants. This variation from the traditional chess set is too much of a change at this stage, but the pieces are beautifully carved and a child is naturally attracted to them and wants to touch them. And so, just as in class I said, "Would you like to dust the India chess set?" and of course the reply was, "Yes!" We do not have a wood-polishing set at home as one would find in a Montessori class, or I would have offered that too.

Matching black and white chess pieces

You will also notice sometimes a very young child is interested in matching the lids to jars or putting the same color of blocks together. This is the mathematical mind at work and it begins very early. For this child you might offer the activity of matching the black and white pieces. Get out one of each: king, queen, castle, bishop, knight, and pawn. Put the six black pieces, in a muddle not a row, on one side of the table and the six white in a muddle on the other side. Select one piece, perhaps the black king, and put it in the middle of the table. Hold your hand over the white pieces as though it were looking for something. Select the white king and carefully place it next to the black king. Don't talk. Remember the child will be able to focus on either your words or your actions, not both at the same time. So allow him to focus on your actions.

Carefully match each of the pieces in a row in the middle of the table. Your goal is to match all of them and then to put them back the way they were on the two sides of the table and invite the child to do the activity, and then when he is finished to put them back and repeat the activity, because repetition is a need of young children and helps them learn. However, if the child is too young to wait for the whole lesson it is natural for him to join you in the work the first time you are matching. Just follow the child.

Chess pieces

King

Queen

Rook
(Castle)

Bishop

Knight

Pawn

Learning the names of chess pieces

Observing children in the first years of life we notice that they are usually working intently on one developmental skill at a time. These can be balance, use of the hand, or language. As he focuses on one, it is as though he lets the other skills rest so he can make great strides in the one he has chosen. It will be very clear if a child is in the stage of interest in language, as he will be trying out new nouns and verbs, and short and long sentences. If the child is in this stage of fascination with language you can teach the names of the chess pieces and this will be very pleasing to the child.

Language is always taught after a child has had experience with the objects or concepts, not before. So it would be taught after the child has been able to see, handle, and perhaps match the chess pieces. The three-period lesson is based on the three stages of learning. As an example one might desire to learn to bake bread. The first stage might be watching someone, reading a recipe of a book on bread baking, or attending a demonstration. The second stage is doing the actual baking. The third stage is the ability to bake the bread without referring to a recipe book, or to teach/show someone else how to bake bread.

In mainstream education all too often the middle stage is left out. Students are required to attend a lecture and take notes, or read an assignment. Then the students are supposed to demonstrate what they have taken in by means of an exam. We are all aware of how long such information stays in our brain. It is definitely not learned in such a way that it will be remembered for a long time. It is the second stage of learning, the practice, the repetition, and the experimentation that fixes new information in the mind.

I remember when my second daughter Ursula, who had been through Montessori 2-6 and 6-12 classes took a middle school class in art history. She came home indignant at what the students had been asked to do,

"We are supposed to write down what the teacher says and read the assignment and then we are going to be given a test on what we learned! What kind of learning is that!" I was so proud that this young lady, at age 13, understood what education can and should be.

The three-period language lesson

In the 3-period lesson for learning the names of chess pieces here are the periods:

First, choose three chess pieces that are all the same color (so the color is not confused in the lesson with the shape) and place them on the table, not on the chessboard. There should be nothing on the table except the three chess pieces. Remember, this should be thought of as a fun activity, not a serious lesson in the traditional sense.

First Period - The child is given the names of three different chess pieces. The name is repeated, the child handed the piece and invited to feel it all over and to repeat the name a few times.

Second Period - The adult provides ways for the child to practice attaching the name and the piece. For example you might say, "Can you hand me the bishop." Or "Can you put the pawn in the corner of the table?" or "Can you hide the king behind your back?" or "Can you put the queen and the knight next to each other." You do this until the child can carry out these actions quickly and without error. If the child makes an error, picks up and moves the wrong piece, you never say, "No, you moved the wrong piece." You just subtly move easily back into the 1st period and repeat the names of all three pieces, moving, handling, naming them, inviting the child to do the same, as though this were a natural part of the game you are playing together.

Third Period – The third period is finding out if he has indeed learned the names of the pieces. You pick up one and say, "What is this chess piece called?" and do the same thing with the other pieces. If the child makes an error in naming you subtly return to the 2nd period to give more practice with you giving the name and the child moving the pieces.

Note: when the child is younger than 2.5, in the stage when most of the language is being internalized from observing others in the environment, and not yet being spoken, we do not ask the child to give the names. So in a Montessori infant community for children from walking to 2.5+ we only give a 2-period lesson. To repeat, the 1st period is our naming and handling the pieces and inviting the child to do the same. The 2nd period is our asking the child to move the pieces about. But we do not ask the child under 2.5 to give us the names of the pieces as we point them out, which is the 3rd period given only to an older child.

The mystery bag, the stereognostic sense

This activity is given after the child has learned the name of the pieces, or is almost finished learning them. The stereognostic sense, in Montessori education, is defined as the ability to distinguish the shape, texture, and consistency of an object by running one's fingers over the object when they cannot be seen with the eyes. This is a combination of tactile and muscular memory that is very strong in the young child who learns by touching. We do this by means of what is called a mystery bag.

Put the chess pieces in their box or container out of sight. Ask the child to choose three different pieces from the box and put them in the bag on the table between you. You should not be able to see what is missing from the box or what the child has chosen. Move the bag close to yourself and put one hand in the bag. Make a great show of handling the different pieces, moving your hands around them, trying to identify them. Finally, say, "Knight?" And then draw the piece out of the bag to see if you have identified the piece correctly. Do this with three all three pieces. Then put them back in the box.

Ask the child, "Would you like me to choose some and you name them?" Then continue with three pieces up to all 6 pieces, repeating as the child chooses.

LEVEL I GAMES, PREPARING THE PLAYING AREA, TAKING TURNS, ENDING A GAME, MOVING ONE PIECE

Preparing the playing area

Before all of the lessons, carefully place only the pieces you are going to use for the lessons on the table, one on each side of the board. Put nothing else on the table to distract the child. At this stage you want him to focus only on the board and the lesson piece. As you set up the playing area move the pieces slowly and carefully and with great attention, as you are the model for the child.

Taking turns

In the chapter on Chess Grace and Courtesy there is a clear explanation of how to teach a child to sit quietly and wait while the chess partner is moving a chess piece. If the child has not already practiced this you could teach it at this point. Of course be sure to model it. The decision of whether or not to teach this now depends on your observation of the child.

Ending a game

Should you be ending the game by shaking hands and saying polite things? This depends on the age of the child, just as did the lesson on taking turns. It is also found in the chapter on Chess Grace and Courtesy. For the very young you might just want to focus on the movement of the king in this first game. You might want to teach how to end the game politely after the first king game, or even later. Or you might want to teach it at a moment when there is no chess game in sight, just as a Montessori grace and courtesy lesson.

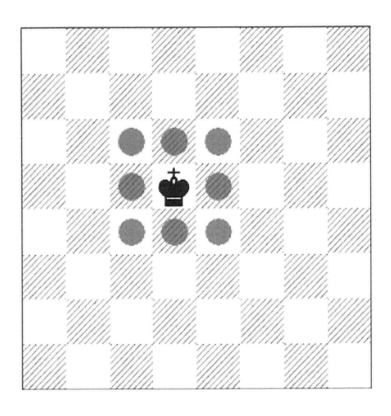

The king game

Materials: The chessboard and both kings

Basic Move Rule: A king can move in any direction, forward, backward, sideways, or diagonally. He can only move one square per move.

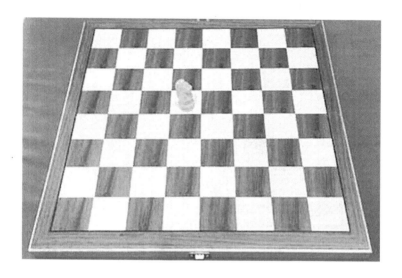

First moves:

1 - Tell the child, "The king can move in any direction, but only to the next square."

2 - Put one of the kings anywhere, on any color square, near the middle of the board, very carefully and slowly placing it in the exact middle of a square.

3 - Offer the child the chance to move the king, "Would you like to move the king to the next square?"

4 - Move the king slowly in another direction.

5 - Invite the child to take a turn.

6 - Do this 3-5 times; depending upon when you think the child understands the move.

7 - Invite the child to move the king the way you did. "Would you like to move the king to the next square?"

8 - If at any time the child moves the king more than one space, don't say anything. Just return to showing him the correct moves when it is again your turn.

9 - Do this until you have moved the king forward, sideways in both directions, backwards, or diagonally.

10 - Each time you move to one of each of these squares place it carefully and slowly, putting the king in the middle of each square. This care of movement will attract the child's interest and serve as a model for all further games. If he does not move a piece as carefully as you do, do not correct or mention it. Remember the Montessori axiom, "Teach by teaching, not by correcting." Continue to model the best way.

11 - Place the king you have been moving to the side of the board and take turns moving this king. This way the child learns that both kings move in the same way.

Ending the lesson:

1 - If it is best to end the lesson or game at this point because the child is very young, tell the child, "When a chess game is finished we shake hands and say thank you."

2 - Hold out your hand, take the child's in yours, and say, "Thank you."

3 - Or you can choose to say, "Thank you for playing chess with me." Or, "I enjoyed our game." Or whatever would be polite and well mannered in your culture.

4 - Show the child how to put the kings and the chessboard away handling everything carefully. This challenges the child in the area of control of movement which is very important, and enjoyed by children at this stage of development.

Ask if that is enough and decide whether to stop the game and shake hands etc. If you are sure the child is ready to go on, invite him to continue with the next piece.

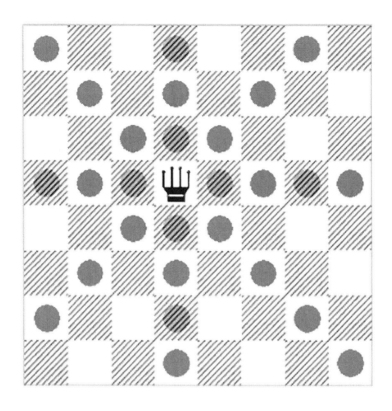

The queen game

Materials: The chessboard and both queens

Basic Move Rule: A queen can move as far as she wants in any direction: forward, backward, sideways, or diagonally. She can only move in one direction per turn.

First moves:

1 - Put one of the queens anywhere near the middle of the board, very carefully and slowly placing it in the middle of a square.

2 - "The queen can move as far as she wants in any direction, but she has to decide which direction she wants to go when it is her turn." Show the child that the queen can move in any direction, just like the king could, but she can go as far as she wants before stopping on a square. You show this by moving the queen in one direction a few squares. As you do this, slowly and carefully move the queen to each square and pausing slightly, before going on. This helps a young child learn to move the piece in a straight line.

3 - "Would you like to move the queen in one direction as far as she wants to go?" Invite the child to move the queen in one direction as you have done. Watch to see if he follows your example of moving one square at a time, putting the piece exactly in the middle of the square, and pausing. If not, do not correct, but be sure he sees how carefully you do this with your next turn.

4 - It is your turn to move the queen. If the child has failed to do part of the move correctly (pausing after moving to the next square, or not placing the queen in the middle of the square) do not mention this, but pay careful attention to doing it correctly with your next turn.

5 - Do this until the child can really understand that the queen can move in any direction, and that she can go 1 square, 2 squares, 3 squares, or more, even to the end of the row. This takes a lot more practice than moving the king, but learning the movement of the king, the only other piece that can move in any direction, has been an important preparation for learning how the queen moves.

6 - When you have moved the queen in all directions, place the queen you have been moving to the side of the board and show the correct moves with the other queen. This way the child learns that both queens move in the same way.

Ending the lesson:

1 - If it is best to end the "game" at this point because the child is very young, tell the child, "When a chess game is finished we shake hands and say 'Thank you.' Or we can say "Nice Game" or "I enjoyed playing chess with you."

2 - Hold out your hand, take the child's in yours, and say one of these polite end-of-game phrases.

3 - If you are sure the child has internalized the movement of the king and queen and is ready to go on, continue with the castle game. Usually learning one or two pieces is enough for a first time, as long as the child knows there will be an opportunity to have another lesson soon. The brain needs some processing time to store the new information.

4 - Together put the queens away and the chessboard away.

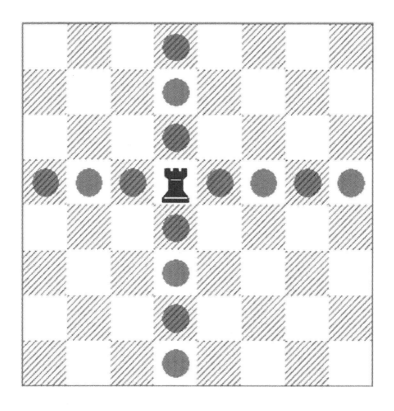

The castle game

Note: This piece is more often called a *rook* for the Sanskrit word for *chariot,* and using the name *castle* is considered old-fashioned, but since it looks like a castle with turrets in the standard chess set this label is easier for children so I always use this name when teaching beginning chess.

Materials: The chessboard and two castles.

Basic Move Rule: A castle can move forward, backwards or sideways, as far as he wants. It cannot move diagonally.

First moves:

1 - Put one of the castles anywhere near the middle of the board, very carefully and slowly placing it in the middle of a square.

2 - "The castle can move as far as it wants, sideways, backwards, or forward." Show the child that the castle can move sideways, forward, or backward – but only one direction for one move.

As you move the castle, just as with all of the other pieces, place it exactly in the middle of the square, and pause, before going on. This helps the child see clearly how to not get off of the path the castle is taking. The child will have learned about moving in only one direction per move with the queen, but it is still worth making the point that the castle can only move one direction per move.

3 - "Would you like to move the castle sideways, forward, or backward as far as he wants to go?" Invite the child to move the castle in one direction, sideways, forward, or backwards. Watch to see if he follows your example of moving one square at a time, putting the piece exactly in the middle of the square, and pausing. If not, do not correct him, but be sure he sees how carefully you do this with your next turn.

4 - Show the child that the castle can move in another direction.

5 - Invite the child to move the castle in another direction.

6 - Do this until you have moved the castle in all three directions, forward, backward, sideways.

7 - Each time you move to one of these squares do it carefully and slowly, putting the castle in the middle of each square. If the student does not move a piece as carefully as you do, do not correct or mention it at that time. Remember the Montessori axiom, "Teach by teaching, not by correcting." And continue to model the best way.

8 - When you have moved the castle in all three directions, place the castle you have been moving to the side of the board and show the correct moves with the other castle. This way the child learns that both castles move in the same way.

Ending the lesson:

1 - If it is best to end the game at this point because the child is very young and the child has learned the polite way to end a game, hold out your hand, take the child's in yours, and say one of the polite end-of-game phrases.

2 - If you are sure the child has internalized the movement of the king, queen, and castle and is ready to go on, continue with the bishop game.

3 - Together put the castles and the chessboard away.

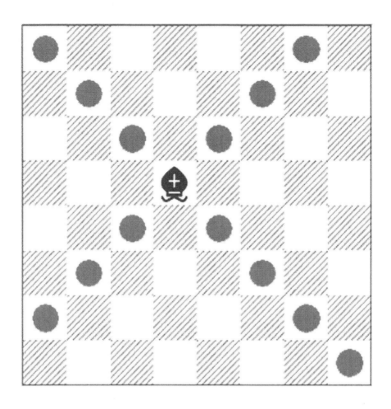

The bishop game

Materials: The chessboard and two bishops

Basic Move Rule: A bishop can move in any diagonal direction as far as he wants, only one direction per move.

First moves:

1 - Introduce the word *diagonal* or *diagonally* because this word is going to be new for most children. "Watch my finger move diagonally." Show the child with your finger on the board what it means to move diagonally. Just as with the chess piece moves above be sure to pause slightly on each square on the path to help make the point that the path is always in a straight line.

2 - You and the child can take turns moving fingers across the board diagonally to make this point. 3 - Observe the child to be sure that he understands the meaning of the word before going on.

4 - Put one of the bishops anywhere near the middle of the board, very carefully and slowly placing it in the middle of a square.

5 - "The bishop can move diagonally as far as he wants." Move the bishop in one diagonal direction to the edge of the board.

6 - Put the bishop back near the center of the board.

7 - "Would you like to move the bishop?"

8 - If the child is confused you can subtly go back to moving diagonally with your finger, or with the bishop piece. Be sure that the child is not made to feel that he has made a mistake.

9 - Continue to take turns moving the bishop. Be sure that you place the bishop exactly in the middle of the each square along his chosen path, and pause, before going on.

10 - Put the bishop back in the middle of the board.

11 - Invite the child to move the bishop as you have done, as far as he wants. Watch to see if he follows your example of moving one square at a time, putting the piece exactly in the middle of the square, and pausing. If not, do not correct, but be sure he sees how carefully you do this with your next turn.

12 - Do this until you have moved the bishop in all four diagonal directions several times.

13 - When you have moved the bishop in all four directions, place the bishop you have been moving to the side of the board and show the correct moves with the other bishop. This way the child learns that both bishops move in the same way.

Ending the lesson:

1 - If it is best to end the "game" at this point hold out your hand, take the child's in yours, and say,

"Thank you" or "Nice Game" or "I enjoyed playing chess with you."

2 - Together put the bishops away and the chessboard away, or let the child do it.

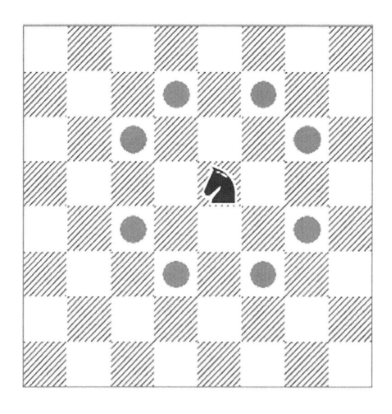

The knight games #1, #2, #3

Note: The movement of the knight is the most complicated part of learning beginning chess. Be sure to watch the child to see that he follows what you are saying and showing, and of course do not move the piece and talk at the same time. This lesson takes a lot of concentration.

Materials: The chessboard and two knights. One other chess piece that the child is familiar with -- the king, queen, castle, or bishop.

Basic Move Rules:

A knight MUST move 1 square in one direction and 2 squares in another direction at a 90-degree angle in one turn. He can move 1 square first or 2 squares first. He cannot move diagonally, just backward, forward, and sideways.

Note: Please practice the knight moves below by yourself, trying each variation several ways. Then if possible try teaching an adult before teaching a child. If there is any confusion on your part while giving a child a lesson, it will create confusion and frustration in the child.

First move #1:

1 - Put one of the knights anywhere near the middle of the board, very carefully and slowly placing it in the middle of a square.

2 - "Each time a knight moves he goes in two directions in one turn." To model this be sure to move one square first and then the 2 squares at a 90% angle

3 - Put the knight back near the middle of the board and show another move, beginning with one square, followed by the two squares at a 90% angle

4 - "Would you like to move the knight?" Letting the child have a turn moving first one square followed by two squares.

5 - Do this, taking turns, several times.

First move #2:

1 - "A knight can move two squares first and then one square." Then show the second way a knight can move, beginning with two squares and followed by moving one square at a 90% angle.

2 - "Would you like to try the second way a knight can move?"

3 - Take turns moving the second way.

4 - Watch to see if he follows your example of moving one square at a time, putting the piece exactly in the middle of the square, and pausing. If not, do not correct, but be sure he sees how carefully you do this with your next turn.

5 - Put the knight back in the middle of the board.

First move #3:

1 - "A knight can do something no other piece can do. He can jump. He can jump over another piece."

2 - Place the second piece you have chosen, let's use the bishop as an example, next to the knight. Show the child how the knight can jump over the bishop. Depending on where the second piece is, the knight will either jump over the bishop making this the 2-square move, then move one square at a 90% angle, or he will move one square first and then turn the 90% angle and jump over the bishop. This sounds confusing but as you

put the pieces out on the board and follow these directions it will make sense.

3 - "Would you like to help the knight jump over the bishop?" Invite the child to do as you have done. You place both pieces and the child moves.

4 - As I said, this is the most confusing piece to teach. So you must use your skills of observation to see how much the child understands and how much he is enjoying the complexity of this piece and be sure that you move on or end the game while he is still interested and has not grown frustrated or tired of chess.

5 - So continue to take turns moving. You can return to moves with no second piece and no jumping, or just practice jumping, or combine the two, "following the child."

6 - When you have practiced just long enough, show a few of the moves with the other knight. Since the child has seen all of the above moves — king, queen, castle, and bishop — with both black and white pieces, this step will be very quick.

Ending the lesson:

1 - If it is best to end the "game" at this point, hold out your hand, take the child's in yours, and say,

"Thank you" or "Nice Game" or "I enjoyed playing chess with you."

2 - Together put the knights away and the chessboard away, or let the child do it.

Note: Pawns are introduced in the next chapter because it is easier and more interesting to introduce all of the pawns at once in their correct placement on the chessboard.

LEVEL I PAWN GAME, INTRODUCING THE PAWNS' PLACE, LEARNING WHO MOVES FIRST, PLAYING THE FIRST PAWN GAME

The Pawn

Materials: The chessboard and all 16 pawns

Basic Move Rule: At this point in learning chess a pawn can only move one square forward. He cannot go sideways, backwards, or diagonally. (There are other pawn moves but they do not concern us at the Level 1 stage of learning chess)

Introducing the Pawn's Place

1 - "Every chess piece has a place where he belongs when a chess game begins. I will show you where the pawns go." Place all of the pawns on the board in their correct place. That means all 8 of the white pawns on the 8 squares on the second row from one edge of the board facing a player, and all of the black pawns on the second row from the opposite edge.

2 - Or you can say you will place the pawns of one color and invite the child to place the other pawns where they go

3 - "A pawn can only go forward one square." Show the child a pawn moving one square forward. And then put the pawn back.

- "Would you like to play a pawn game?"

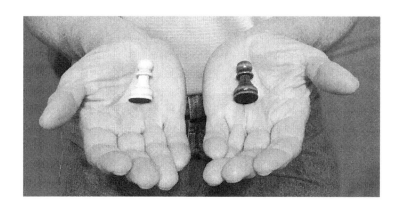

Who moves first?

1 - If the child says, "yes." Say, "Okay, first I will show you how a chess game begins."

2 - Tell the child, "In chess the person who is using the white pieces always moves first."

3 - Remove one black pawn and one white pawn from the board.

4 - Put them in your hands behind your back.

5 - Put your hands in front of you, between you and the child and tell him, "One hand contains the white pawn and the other the black pawn. You can choose one."

6 - If he has chosen the white pawn rotate the board on the table so the white pawns are on the second row on his side and he will move first.

7 - If he has chosen the black pawn the black pawns will be on his side and you will move first.

The first pawn game

1 - Replace the pawns that were in your hand so all 16 are on the board in the correct positions.

2 - Move any one of your pawns 1 square forward.

3 - Invite the child to move one of his pawns.

4 - Be sure that you are not talking, have your mouth closed, and your hands in your lap, when he is moving his pawn.

5 - Each time you move to one of each of these squares do it carefully and slowly, putting the pawn in the middle of each square. If he does not move a piece as carefully as you do, do not correct or mention it. Remember the Montessori axiom, "Teach by teaching, not by correcting." And continue to model the best way.

Soon the pawns will have moved as far as they can, and each one will be "facing" or right next to the partner's pawns. Since the pawns look a little bit like little people I have heard some delightful comments by children at this point. "Hello, how are you today?" or "Thank you for playing chess with me." And "It is nice to see you." It is clear to me since the comments, the children's imaginary conversations between the black and white pawns, have already been positive and polite, they are associating these emotions with the learning of chess if courtesy is being taught.

Then you can invite the child to do it again. With an older child you can even introduce the pawn rule #2 at this point which is, "On the first move a pawn can move two squares or one square. But only on the first move." But it is fine to wait. Or you can invite him to help you put the pieces away carefully, or go on to the next game. If you are going to end the session don't forget to offer your hand and say one of the polite comments traditional for ending a real chess game.

LEVEL 1 GAMES, LEARNING THE CORRECT PLACES OF ALL OF THE PIECES, PLAYING 2-PIECE AND 3- PIECE GAMES

Learning the correct places of all of the pieces

Materials: The chessboard and all of the chess pieces

Basic Move Rule: Each chess piece will follow the rules learned in the games in Chapters 6 and 8. The pawn will either move one or two squares forward on their first move.

1 - Put all of the white pieces next to the board at one end and all of the black pieces next to the board at the other end.

2 - Place all of the white pieces on the board in their correct places in the following order.

3 - Place all of the pawns the second row from the edge of the board as the child has already learned.

4 - Select the 4 castle pieces. Say "The castles go in the corners and all of the other pieces are inside the castle or between the two castles." You place for example the two white castles in their corners, in the first row behind the pawns, and invite the child to place the two black castles

5 - Select the queens and say, "The queen goes on her color." Show the child by placing the white queen in the middle of the first row on the white (not-black) square, behind the row of white pawns. Invite the child to place the black queen on the opposite side of the board, on the black square in the middle of the first row behind the black pawns.

6 - Select the kings and say, "The king goes next to the queen." Show the child by placing the white king in the middle of the first row, on the black square next to the white queen. Invite the child to place the black king

in the middle of the other first row next to the black queen

7 - Select the bishops and say, "The bishops go next to the king and queen." And place the two white bishops next to the king and queen. Invite the child to do the same with the black bishops.

8 - Select the knights and say, "The knights go next to the castles." And place the two white knights next to the white castles. Invite the child to place the black knights next to the black castles.

Now you have shown how to place all of the pieces in the correct place. With an older child you can begin to play what looks like a real chess game by taking turns moving the pieces in the way you have learned. This is not a competition, not a game to put pieces "in check" or to "check mate" the king. It is still just learning how the pieces move, and practice moving them. It can be very interesting. Be sure to go through the step of deciding who gets white and begins the game.

Playing 2-piece games

For a younger child you can now play "2-piece" games. This is how it works:

1 - Say, "Let's play a game with two kinds of pieces. I choose the pawns and the knights." (Or you can choose any two pieces – but be sure you have practiced this alone or with an adult beforehand so you know the possibilities).

2 - Together remove all of the pieces except the ones you have decided to use for a 2-piece game. Place them carefully, standing up and not on their sides, next to the board as they were.

3 - Go through the "who gets white and moves first" step. Pick two pawns, one black and one white, and put them behind your back then in front of the child to

choose one. Or if the child is ready, invite him to do this and you choose.

4 - Adjust the board so that the white pieces are directly in front of the child if he chooses white, and in front of you if he chose black.

5 - Whoever has the white pieces makes the first move. I like the pawn-knight game because it is fun to show the knights (on horses) jump over the pawns. The pawns will continue to move only forward and the knights can go wherever they like. There is no goal except for the practice in moving the pieces correctly.

6 - The game can end whenever you both like. It is quite often that as soon as the child understands the variety of moves he will want to do another game with two different pieces.

7 - Sometimes it is best to keep one of the pieces you just used and only one different piece in the next game, such as king-pawn, or knight-queen.

8 - Before the child gets tired say, "Wow, we have played a lot of chess. Is that enough for one day?"

9 - Shake hands, say something polite to each other, and help put the board and pieces away.

Playing 3-piece games

Sometimes the next stage is to follow all of the directions for the 2-piece games but playing 3-piece games with any 3 pieces. When the child is ready to practice moves with all of the moves he is ready to learn how to remove the partner's pieces from the board.

THE AMSTERDAM CHESS MUSEUM AND REMOVING OR CAPTURING A PARTNER'S PIECE FROM THE BOARD

The Amsterdam Chess Museum

I was very fortunate when researching for this book to visit the Chess Museum in Amsterdam. Machgielis "Max" Euwe, PhD (1901 – 1981), shown above in 1066 with his wife and grandchildren, was a Dutch chess Grandmaster, mathematician, and author. He won every Dutch chess championship that he participated in from 1921 until 1952, and additionally won the title in 1955 – his 12 titles are still a record. He published a mathematical analysis of the game of chess from an intuitive point of view, in which he showed that the then-official rules did not exclude the possibility of infinite games.

The chess museum, Max Euwe Centrum, was created shortly after his death and serves as a museum and a provider of training courses in both advanced chess and computer, provides seminars and conferences for those interested in the cultural, social and academic aspects of chess. They were extremely helpful to me in creating this book. For example, when it comes to teaching a child about how to "take" a chess partner's piece off of the board. I always had a problem, as it was a leap from learning the moves of the pieces together with a partner, to competing to win a game.

Removing or capturing a partner's piece

Materials: The chessboard, a checkers piece or small coin, and one chess piece at a time. Select any chess piece except the pawn.

"Opstapje I" is the name of the book I was given at the chess museum. Two Dutch Montessori students translated it for me so I could better explain it. In the picture above you see two pictures from the book. The funny one gives an idea of the sense of humor throughout all of these books. The second one shows a knight and a checkers piece on the board. The goal is to see how one can move the chess piece to the checkers piece.

When he lands on the checkers piece IT IS REMOVED FROM THE BOARD. This is so simple. For older children, this landing on the square which is occupied by a partner's piece and removing it from the board is called *capturing*. But for now we can just say we are removing it.

Looking at the illustration, we can see that the knight can move several ways in order to land on the checker in two moves. But if the child wants to, he can move the knight all over the board before landing on the checker. You can show the child how to do this, making all of the moves yourself, or take turns with the child moving the knight until it lands on the checker. Or with an older child you can challenge him to see what is the fastest way to get to the checker.

What follows is up to you and the student. Invite the child to pick the next piece and together you will make a lot of discoveries. For example, the king will take a long time since he can only move one square at a time. Have fun.

Depending on his age and stage of development, you might want to move the pieces one square at a time, and emphasize putting your hands in your lap and being still when it is his turn. But be sure to finish the game politely

The Pawn: There is a special rule for how a pawn captures, or removes a partner's piece. We know that the first move of the pawn is either one or two squares forward. From then on the pawn can only move one square forward. However, in order to land on a piece or capture a piece, he must move one square diagonally onto that square. This comes in the next chapter.

LEVEL 2 GAMES, INTRODUCING THE CONCEPTS OF CHECK AND CHECKMATE, THE 3RD PAWN MOVE, HELPING EACH OTHER

Introducing the concepts of *check* and *checkmate*

Level 2 chess is a real chess game and the whole world of chess begins to open up at this point. The goal of all traditional chess games is to get one's pieces into positions so that the partner's king will be removed or captured in the next move, and there is no place for him to move to avoid this, and it is not possible for one of his other pieces to help him. Interestingly the word checkmate is thought to come from Persia, where the game had spread from India. *Shah* is the word for king and *mat* meant helpless or defeated. So *Shah mat*, which became *checkmate*, means the king is defeated. This kind of information will attract the child above the age of 6 when the interest in history and etymology is the foundation for Montessori education at this age.

To be *in check* means to be in danger of being removed by one's chess partner in the next move. When a king is *in check* he must do something about this in the next move. In some places it is considered polite to tell a chess partner when a king is in check. In other places it is considered rude. Checkmate means that the king will be taken in the next move, no matter what is done. The player who has put him in checkmate does not remove the king, the losing chess partner merely lays his king down on the square where he was standing.

When our second grandchild Tai was 4 years old and visiting us in California from Portland, Oregon, a friend, a teenage girl, visited us and Tai asked her if she would like to play chess. They sat on the sofa for some time playing and at the end of the game Tai came to me with such a sad face and said, "She didn't play level two." The teenager looked at me in some confusion because she didn't like seeing Tai so sad and said, "I have never heard of 'level two'. What does that mean?" And so I explained.

In 2015, I was in Mongolia to give the first AMI Montessori public lectures and to consult with two schools. I was staying with a family who had a 5-year-old boy whose grandfather had taught him the chess moves. One evening that the boy and his father were playing chess in the living room, Ermuun suddenly exploded into anger, stomping and yelling and his father looked toward me with a puzzled look on his face. I asked what happened and the father said, rather sadly, "He doesn't like to lose." My reply was that winning and losing was not appropriate at this age, but the emphasis is better placed on spending fun time with one's father, and learning more and more about chess. And, with his interest aroused I went on to explain the "Three Levels of Chess" that our family has developed over the years.

Later I received news from Mongolia that the boy enjoys chess now much more than before.

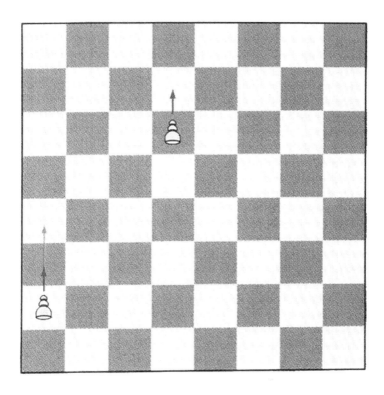

The pawn removing or capturing a partner's piece

So far the child learned where the pawns go on the board, and that they can only move forward one square at a time. He probably also learned that for the move, and only for the first move, a pawn can move two spaces forward. As in the picture above.

It is a simple step for the child who has learned everything that has come before this step to understand that in order for a pawn to remove or capture a partner's piece he must move onto that chess pieces square diagonally. Depending on the child you can practice this just a few times, or more.

The pawn being promoted,

or "Queening the Pawn"

This is another pawn move that is very important when playing a real game. The rule is that when a pawn makes it all the way to the first row of the partner's side of the board, he can ask that this pawn be promoted into whatever piece he chooses except a king. Since the queen is the most powerful piece, she is usually chosen. This is possible even if the queen is still on the board. That means that a piece that has been removed, such as a castle or bishop, can be called a queen and have the power of a queen. This special move is called "Queening the Pawn" no matter what piece the player chooses to exchange for his pawn.

The above new rules are the only ones necessary for playing a real game.

Helping each other

Keep in mind throughout this chapter that the main point in this stage is to help each other, not to compete with each other.

Advanced chess rules

There are other rules, but by this point you will easily be able to make sense of any beginning chess book and try out these for yourself. In my life I have very seldom used them. But here they are.

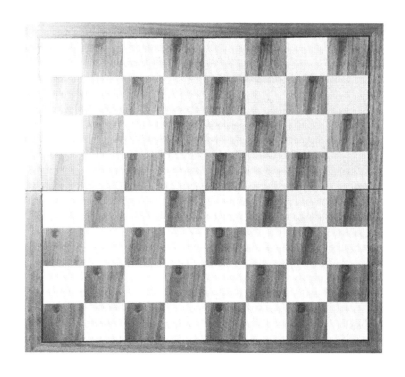

Proper setting of the chessboard

Proper setting of the chessboard should be placed so that the right hand corner of the first row of each player is white (or pale colored)

Chess notation

The horizontal rows are called *ranks*, and the vertical rows are called *files*. Letters and numbers identify them. There are different kinds of notation but that is something you can choose to learn later. However, if notation is learned, it makes it easy to play chess at a distance. The chess pieces are represented by initials: Pawn-P; Knight-N or Kt; Bishop-B; Castle or Rook-R; Queen-Q; King-K. As an example you can email a friend that you have moved a certain piece from one square to another by notating the initial of the piece and the rank and file of the first and second position.

Castling

This is a special move where a king and a castle can change places. In competitive chess this is a very important possibility. Here are the rules about when one cannot castle: (1) If there is a piece standing between the king and the castle; (2) if the king or castle have already moved; (3) if the king is in check; (4) if the king has to cross a square guarded by the chess partner's piece; (5) if the king will be in check after castling. I have only used castling a few times in my life, but then I play for fun and learning, not competitively.

En Passant

This is a special pawn move. *En passant* is French for "in passing." If a player moves a pawn two squares in an opening move, the chess partner is allowed to remove/capture it by one of his own pawns as though it had only moved one square. But this must be done on immediately following the movement of the first pawn. Personally I have never used this move and find it difficult. But it is good to know if you or your student really want to master this move.

Chess books

At this point in learning chess, you will find that you the teacher and even a young child will enjoy looking through chess books that have been written for children. Adults and children alike will enjoy the variety of chess sets that have been created over the years.

LEVEL 3 GAMES, TRYING TO WIN
ON ONE'S OWN

Remember, the overriding importance of Level 2 chess is that we help the student who is receiving the lessons learn how to think ahead, make intelligent moves, and enjoy these things so they will be applied in other situations. This kind of thinking is valuable throughout life. The official goal of winning or beating someone else is secondary!

Make this level of learning chess fun, even though it is the beginning of competitive chess. For example you can play two games at once as in the above picture. When I did this with our two oldest grandchildren, it felt a bit like a Montessori class, because all three of us were involved in making the best and most thoughtful games we could while working together.

At some point you can ask, "Would you like to play a game where we both try to get each other's kings checkmated and don't help each other?" The answer might surprise you. Even though traditional grading systems and competition do not form part of a Montessori education, children like to set goals for themselves. For example, years ago, teaching Montessori 6-12 classes I realized that Montessori students often excel in all areas of math except speed of reciting the multiplication tables. The end of 6th grade California state exams showed this. So I asked the students what we could do about this. They created a method of using a stopwatch to test each other, to identify and help each other learn the combinations that caused the most difficulty. They quickly mastered this part of the California state tests. There are many examples of Montessori students going way beyond what is required of them when challenged and in charge of their own methods and results. So don't be surprised if they take on this challenge in chess.

Personally I love to help a person see a good move, and to be helped to see one I might have missed, even if I am playing a level 3 game, or trying to win. This is the Montessori way of teaching and learning, no matter what the age of the student. And what a world we would live in if all planning for the future or problem solving were handled in this way.

THE QUESTION OF COMPETITION

Cooperative or non-competitive board games

Over the years we have become aware of a wonderful cooperative game movement that supports Montessori cooperative education and thinking. Games such as "Harvest Time" can be played by parents and their children as young as three or four. To play, 2-4 players work together to bring in the harvest before the cold weather sets in. When one is finished gathering in his own crops, he turns to help the other players. This kind of game sets the tone for the spirit of beginning chess, and skills for real life.

I highly recommend the website www.familypastimes.com. Family Pastimes games are the inventions of Jim Deacove who started making co-operative games for his own family, and was encouraged by friends to make them widely available. This was in 1972. Today they are known around the globe. Here is an article from their website: Cooperative Games: A way to modify aggressive behavior in young children

From a study in The Journal of Applied Behavior Analysis: We investigated the effects of competitive and cooperative games on aggressive and cooperative behaviors of 70 children (4 to 5 years old) from four classes in three preschools. The experimental design included both multiple baseline and reversal components. Behaviors were measured during game conditions and in subsequent free-play periods. Results showed that cooperative behavior increased and aggression decreased during cooperative games; conversely, competitive games were followed by increases in aggressive behavior and decreases in cooperative behavior. (See the website for the complete study)

This book is a Montessori favorite:

No Contest: The Case Against Competition,

by Alfie Kohn

Archery in Bhutan

A few years ago in Bhutan I watched an archery competition. Just before one person, either man or woman, was about to release the arrow from his bow, someone would crack a joke or try to distract him in some way and everyone present would double over in laughter. And whenever someone would hit a bull's-eye, all of the archers would line up and dance! Bhutan is famous for its goal of GNH (Gross National Happiness) rather than GDP (Gross Domestic Product), and the way they approach sports, as a humorous and fun part of life rather then fierce and serious competition, reflects this.

From the very beginning of a Montessori education, a child is given the opportunity to help another or to be helped by another child. Even a one-year-old learns to set the table, setting a place for each of his friends. And when one is finished with a project, such as polishing wood, the reason he masters cleaning everything up and putting it away is so that it will be ready for the next child. This is high-level socialization and cooperation. Early in life children learn to give lessons to each other and at the 6-12+ level spontaneous groups form to do research and then make presentations to fellow classmates.

In this non-competitive, cooperative system of education children's learning is enjoyable and it is remembered. Nothing is memorized for a text, but because children are given the tools and freedom to explore information far beyond the knowledge of the teacher, they feel good about their learning. This love of learning, or exploring and carrying out research, and working together to meet a goal is real preparation for life. Since everything is changing so fast these days the traditional curriculum that worked for so long is no longer valuable. The skills needed are just those that are found in Montessori schools, which is why well-trained Montessori teachers and teacher-trainers are in great demand. It is cooperation that is going to create a better world.

THE EVOLUTION OF CHESS, CREATIVITY, BENEFITS OF CHESS

Some examples of chess pieces

through history and the world

The game of chess has been around for over 1,000 years. It is thought by most to have begun in India. But some say the precursor of chess began as early as 2,000 years ago in Ancient Afghanistan. Historians tell us that in India there was a game called *chuturanga* which means "four sections of the military" which were at that time the infantry (foot soldiers, like today's chess pawns), the cavalry (perhaps present day knights, as they are sometimes shown on horseback), the *elephantry*, and the *chariotry* (common means of transportation still today in parts of India. Even today there are being produced beautifully carved sets in India, with the traditional images of kings and queens, which were called in Sanskrit *Maharaja* (great ruler or high king) and *Maharani* (great queen).

There is an amazing variety of chess sets that have been created throughout history — the pieces representing horses, camels, yaks, soldiers, and abstract art, depending on the country and the century. Beginning at age 6 or 7 in the Montessori elementary class, the child begins the study of history. The study of the history of language is a favorite subject in Montessori elementary classes and it follows the spread of civilizations, of migrations, trade, improvements in transportation vehicles, language, and games.

The Lewis chessmen were discovered in early 1831 in a sand bank on the west coast of the Isle of Lewis, in the Outer Hebrides of Scotland. There are various local stories concerning their discovery, but it is clear that they were carved from walrus ivory and whale tooth between around 1150 and 1200. When found, some were stained red, suggesting that the original color combination of the pieces was red and white. The pieces that probably raise the biggest smiles are the famously grumpy queens who rest their chins in their hands, nursing a toothache or fretting about the weather. The movie version of the book *Harry Potter and the Philosopher's Stone* has made this set famous and inspired a new interest in chess in young people.

The spread of the game of chess followed the same path. From India the game probably spread, along with other trade goods carried on the silk route, to Persia (present day Iran). And when the Arabs moved into Persia it began to spread throughout the Arab world. When the Arabs conquered Persia, chess was taken up by the Muslim world and subsequently spread to Eastern Southern Europe. It also spread all over Russia and Eastern Europe. There are several theories of why there have always been so many excellent chess players in Russia.

Chess was subsidized during the Soviet Union era because it was cheap, and anyone could play it. Another theory is that traditional education in Russia is based on the way the brain works in even the youngest children; instead of education for tests, the focus is an awareness of patterns, and of analyzing the steps of learning, building slowly, which is called "the art of analysis."

I think this is a bit like the Montessori way of learning how to learn, rather than valuing a curriculum-centered education.

Creativity - Oden's game

Chess has changed many times since its birth in India and it is still changing. The rules have changed and why cannot children continue to change them? Recently I was playing chess with my sister's grandchildren. One the youngsters, already identified as a unique and creative thinker, decided to make up his own game. I had given them a combination chess and checkers set and he wanted to created a way to use all of the pieces of both sets in one game.

I explained that all games were the result of agreement between people about how the game is played. An example is the rules of Scrabble in our family. Scrabble is a word game in which two to four players score points by placing tiles, each bearing a single letter, onto a game board which is divided into a 15×15 grid of squares. The tiles must form words which, in crossword fashion, flow left to right in rows or downwards in columns. The words must be defined in a standard dictionary. The game is played without access to a dictionary unless a word is being challenged.

But a year ago I suggested that this way of playing limits the players to words they already know, so our family began to play with the dictionary as our constant companion, accessible at any time. This was a cooperative way of playing, and it was so exciting for all of us to learn so many new words in one game that winning became secondary. It was still fun to find words that could score a lot of points and have a high score at the end of the game, but there was much more learning and enjoyment of Scrabble from then on.

So why not a game with chess pieces and checkers together? All I remember, as I heard him explain his new game to his brother and cousin, was "And the Queen has more power when she is standing on a checker!"

Benefits of chess

I once came across a list of 10 ways learning chess can benefit the brain. Here is the list:

- It increases creativity

- It improves memory

- It increases problem-solving skills

- It can raise an IQ

- It grows dendrites

- It can help prevent Alzheimer's

- It exercises both sides of the brain

- It improves reading skills

- It improves concentration

- It teaches planning and foresight

These are all important results of learning chess. But in learning chess the Montessori way we can add to this list:

- It helps one learn patience

- It teaches body awareness and grace

- It teaches good manners

- It teaches cooperative problem solving

- It teaches how to help another

- It teaches one how to treat another person the way one would like to be treated

And maybe you can think of even more.

CONCLUSION AND THANK YOU

This book comes from almost 50 years of exploring ways of sharing chess and life with children in ways that are fun, funny, thoughtful, purposeful, and that help both parties learn and thrive. It was a surprise to me that wherever and whenever I mentioned the possibility of creating such a book people have requested to pre-order copies. Often these requests have been from adults who had never learned chess, or who thought it would be too difficult, or who wanted to learn along with their children. I would like to give a special thank you to these people who pushed me to finish it. I would also like to thank all those people who let me practice on them as I tried to write down things I had been doing for years but never had explained to another adult. And most of all I am grateful to friends and family who volunteered to proof this and my other books. And, even though she is no longer with us, I am thankful to my dear friend Karin Salzmann, without whose encouragement and help I would never have written anything.

It is my hope that learning chess will be more than just another required skill to master for children who, in our culture at least, are already over-scheduled and in need of time to relax, think, play, and spend unplanned time with friends and family. I hope that the ideas in this book will be a model for all of us to continue to come up with ways of sharing our favorite activities and spending quality and enjoyable time with children.

ABOUT THE AUTHOR

In 1963-1964 Susan Mayclin Stephenson spent four months aboard the first university on shipboard traveling around the world and studying the cultures of Europe, the Middle East, and Asia. This awakened a life-long interest in cultures of the world, specifically concerning the education of children from birth on. She has degrees in philosophy and education, three AMI (Association Montessori Internationale) diplomas: 0-3 years, 2.5-3 years, and 6-12 years, and over 40 years of teaching experience. In 2001 Susan took a course on Multiple, from Dr. Howard Gardner, at Harvard, University to help her understand the variety of learning styles she had seen catered to in Montessori classes. Susan has traveled in over 60 countries and often shares these experiences in oil paintings. She has taught ages 2-17, worked with parents and teachers, consulted with schools, and served as an examiner on Montessori training courses. For more about Susan's work see the link to her blog at www.susanart.net

Made in the USA
San Bernardino, CA
25 March 2016